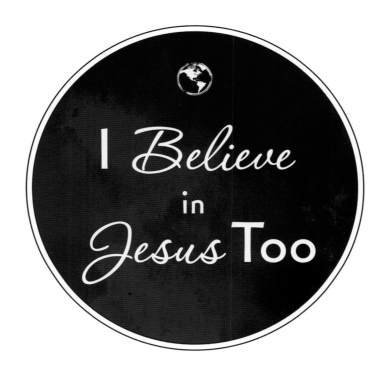

I Believe in Jesus Too

WRITTEN BY **MARK S. NIELSEN**

ILLUSTRATED BY **CRAIG STAPLEY**

DESERET BOOK

SALT LAKE CITY, UTAH

To my parents who taught me to Believe,
to my wife, Anne, who Believes in me,
and to my children, may you always Believe.
—M.S.N.

To all God's children in whom
believing comes so naturally. May
the rest of us follow their example.
—C.S.

Text © 2012 Mark S. Nielsen
Illustrations © 2012 Craig Stapley

Visit us at DeseretBook.com

Library of Congress Cataloging-in-Publication Data

Nielsen, Mark S. author.
  I believe in Jesus too / Mark S. Nielsen; illustrated by Craig Stapley.
    pages cm
  Summary: "*I Believe in Jesus Too* celebrates all the ways that Latter-day Saint children around the world worship Jesus Christ"—Provided by publisher.
  ISBN 978-1-60908-741-8 (hardbound : alk. paper)
  1. Mormon children—Religious life—Juvenile literature. 2. Jesus Christ—Juvenile literature. 3. Faith—Juvenile literature.
  I. Stapley, Craig (Craig Delbert), 1978– illustrator. II. Title.
  BV4571.3.N54 2011
   248.3—dc23   2011013302

Printed in China   1/2012
Four Colour Print Group, Nansha, China

10 9 8 7 6 5 4 3 2 1

Latter-day Saint children everywhere in the world believe in Jesus Christ.

I believe in Jesus too.

Because we believe in Jesus, we go to church on Sunday.

In the United States, Sam rides the New York City subway to church with his family.

In Tonga, Sela walks along the beach to get to church.

Pablo walks through the rain forest to go to church in Bolivia.

In Finland, Katri drives by beautiful snowcapped mountains on her way to church.

Children go to church in many different types of church buildings.

In Russia, Dimitri attends church in an apartment building.

Lani's church building in Fiji is made out of coconut trees.

In Spain, María's chapel is small but beautiful.

Alyssa attends church in a big California meetinghouse in the United States.

THE CHURCH OF
JESUS CHRIST
OF LATTER-DAY SAINTS

Children from
all over the world
sing, pray, and read
scriptures in many
different languages.

In Mexico, Manuel sings Primary songs in Spanish.

In Kenya, Imani prays in Swahili.

In the Philippines, Bayani reads scriptures in Tagalog.

In Taiwan, Ming reads with his Primary class in Mandarin.

Children all over
the world love
family home evening.

In Japan, Junpei enjoys a family home
evening lesson in a tall skyscraper.

In Australia, Kylie plays a family home evening game in the Outback.

Emeka says a family home evening prayer in a small hut in Nigeria.

Claire eats a family home evening treat in a nice warm cabin in Canada.

Following the example of Jesus, children all over the world are baptized.

In Jamaica, Shamara was baptized in the ocean.

In the Netherlands, Maarten was baptized in a beautiful church font filled with warm water.

João was baptized in a cold river in Brazil.

Children all over the world love Jesus,
and He loves them. They believe in
Jesus, and I believe in Jesus too.

What about you?